Everything Has Ears
and
Everything Has a
Womb

What are you Hearing and Birthing?

Annette Red Wilson

Everything Has Ears and Everything Has a Womb
What are you Hearing and Birthing?

Published by TaylorMade Publishing
Jacksonville, FL
www.TaylorMadePublishingFL.com
(904) 323-1334

TaylorMade Publishing

God gives life and

God allows death.

God will root up and

God will plant again,

He speaks it and so it is.

Trust God and Live.

Table of Contents

Introduction i

Dedications iv

Chapter 1: It is Yours For the Asking 1

Chapter 2: Reclaiming and Redirecting Your Lighted Life.. 7

Chapter 3: They Are Listening 17

Chapter 4: Look Around – You Will See What You Created
.... 21

Acknowledgement... 28

About the Author 29

Introduction

All thanks and praise go to God Almighty!

I was given the desire to author this book in 2007. I delayed writing this book because I was trying to be perfect. This interfered with me being authentic which caused me to not write at all. Today, I embrace my space as a writer.

In this book, you will see that words are spirit and they are life. We can command our words and our spirit. If we do not, someone else will. I pray that this work empowers you to be all God called you to be and speak God's truth in life as your ever-growing authentic self.

Everything Has EARs and Everything Has a Womb...

I spoked to my mind which heard me,

shaped me, and gave life to me,

from the decrees of my God,

given me power which echoes in my soul.

Fantastic thoughts, and purpose that oozed out of me.

because I spoke and gave birth.

I have spoken words of power to my dreams,

and they came forth bold of the first
cry of my words...

I am here!

Where shall I go out to make a difference?

Woo wee my destiny heard me and

I am here making a difference!

Did not I say that everything has ears,

and everything has a womb.

Yes man, I came from you and

heard God say come forth and

you manifested me from your Rib,

and you gave birth to me...

I heard your name for me.

"WOMAN"

out of the rib of your womb,

I came forth.

Dedications

To my parents Roosevelt & Mary Wilson,

who are resting in heaven, and to my beautiful
daughters, Erica and Kayla Franklin.

Thank you, Theresa White, for your
encouraging words,

"you are someone everybody needs to hear."

To all those who will read this book – Thank you!

Chapter 1: It is Yours For the Asking

Ask and you shall receive, seek you shall find knock and the door shall be opened, keep on asking, keep on seeking and keep on knocking!

It's Yours For the Asking!

The black force of my tongue declares greatness,

*my tongue that will form it sharps and radiates
colors the reds,*

*yellows, greens the mixtures of golds it is endless.
as the sky,*

*the earth and my being that flows with joy,
prosperity, and peace,*

great health only good and greatness can be seen

because the forces of my tongue give birth

out of the blackness comes the light

and out of darkness comes light.

The tongue has a powerful force that can bring life
or death, when one speaks, it forms a vibration that
can make or break the situation, circumstance that
produce the manifestation of spoken words,
thoughts, and deeds. We must consciously and
intentionally speak purely in the right direction.

I want to help remind us to come back to WHO we
really are, and not who they say we are. Who are

we? Right here I want to answer that one question that is always getting asked.

Who are they? They are those who will try to kill your purpose, want you to bow down and worship them. They are the ones who will steal your identity, kick you out of a room that you are divinely sent to show up in, and they will do it by any means necessary. They are those who shamelessly want to manipulate and control in order to dominate your very being. I can go on; I hope you get the point.

Therefore, it is important for you to know who you are. Listen, the signs are in you to show you who you are, and the most visible sign that is in you is God Himself. It is important that you do not get distracted by "them". Whoever or whatever YOU say you are, you will be. Many others, a person, a system, might take every opportunity to tell you who you are. But it is only when YOU receive what they say of you, you become what they say. Your being has Ears, so Declare your functions and attributes today and watch you become a greater You.

I am fantastic, and peaceful, I am making and doing productive things, helping myself and others in my

life today. I will not back down from Being Great, I am the success in my own life.

Birth a new you today and shake off the old negative mindset that was spoken over you to derail, sabotage, and keep you in a fog. Say and do something differently, Why? By doing so it may cost you. Knowing that it may cost you, you must level up within yourself. The return will make you rich spiritually, mentally, emotionally, and so on.

I ask What are you Speaking? The mouth is only saying what is in your Heart and Mind. What you speak will cause the ears of it to hear and come through the womb of something. We know it takes nine months for a baby to be born. We also know that some babies can be born prematurely and cause all types of insecurities and mental challenges to the one who is giving birth and the baby being birthed. See, the things we say do not just affect us, but has the potential to affect all that is connected to us.

A man's words can be affective 1000 miles (about 1609.34 km) away, how much closer it can affect our life. My baby was born before the set time of nine months due to my misdirected words. I gave birth twice; one was full term and one was premature. For

some selfish reason I spoke the Month and Date I wanted my baby to be born, unconnected to reality, I was speaking to have a premature baby.

Yes, it was a selfish reason I wanted my daughter to be born on a certain date and she was. It was a scary time for me because she was born premature. Her heart was still dependent on me and not fully developed yet. She was no longer in me, and her heart would skip beats and not at a normal pace. All because I lacked understanding and knowledge.

I had her on the exact month and date I had spoken. After she was born, we were tasked with taking a Heart monitoring machine home with us that would track the heart beat patterns which would alert us if her heart stopped. It was crazy because that machine seems to go off every 30 seconds and it was causing us all sorts of mental anguish. I was careless with my words. I went on a fast, prayed and declared that we were going to return that machine back to the doctor and she was going to be healed.

Today, she is whole! I have learned what happens when one Speak and ask for things unconsciously and without knowledge. When we do not wait on

the divine set principle of the almighty God, there could be repercussions.

Please understand that every word, thought and deed will potentially affect everything and everyone that is connected to you. Habitually ignoring or being unaware of your words, thoughts and deeds will continue to cause a state of misfortune. For example, closing a business too soon, divorcing or entering marriage covenant for all the wrong reasons. I can go on and on. However, I know that you get the point.

We must learn and abide by the principles of God's word. Therefore, we must change and speak to the wombs of our divine destiny. As a man thinks, so is he. There is life and death in the power of your words.

Chapter 2: Reclaiming and Redirecting Your Lighted Life

I Will Not Abandon My Position

Abandon my post, for what?

Draw back for what?

Only if it is wise for me!

To share in the fake school of thought

that someone does not think I can, or I will.

You must know NOW,

that it is not what you think,

it is my thoughts that removes adversity,

or brings advantages.

So, I remain cemented in my position.

I will not abandon my post,

just because the blockers are standing in the way.

Through my experiences I have learned

my mind is greater than the blockers.

I Stand Still and see the salvation of the Lord.

I am not alone.

We are in the position to reclaim and redirect our lives, with well-defined chosen words, deeds, and actions. Oftentimes we allow ourselves to be double crossed by arrogance, doubt, fear and the demonic which causes us to remove ourselves from a space of success because we deviated from God's power, truth, and divine guidance.

When we find ourselves in unwanted spaces and situations that do not align with the truth, it is a sign that it is time to reclaim our success. We need to turn back, redirect and reclaim the success which is assigned to our destiny. Yet, we must first come to know that we were double crossed. Then, we can recover from the hurt, shame, humiliation, and the unwanted situations. When we are selected for greatness one cannot remain in hurt, shame, or humiliation. Therefore, in turning back one may need to employ repentance.

When employing repentance, I am talking about taking responsibility for your actions, and move forward in integrity. This is the element of turning back that I am speaking of. If you are having difficulty employing repentance or redirecting your life, then reading Daniel chapter 4 will assist you.

This is the account of Nebuchadnezzar's Dream of a Tree

King Nebuchadnezzar, To the nations and peoples of every language, who live in all the earth: May you prosper greatly!

2 It is my pleasure to tell you about the miraculous signs and wonders that the Most High God has performed for me.

3 How great are his signs, how mighty his wonders! His kingdom is an eternal kingdom; his dominion endures from generation to generation.

4 I, Nebuchadnezzar, was at home in my palace, contented and prosperous.

5 I had a dream that made me afraid. As I was lying in bed, the images and visions that passed through my mind terrified me.

6 So I commanded that all the wise men of Babylon be brought before me to interpret the dream for me.

7 When the magicians, enchanters, astrologers and diviners came, I told them the dream, but they could not interpret it for me.

8 Finally, Daniel came into my presence, and I told him the dream. (He is called Belteshazzar, after the name of my god, and the spirit of the holy gods is in him.)

9 I said, "Belteshazzar, chief of the magicians, I know that the spirit of the holy gods is in you, and no mystery is too difficult for you. Here is my dream; interpret it for me.

10 These are the visions I saw while lying in bed: I looked, and there before me stood a tree in the middle of the land. Its height was enormous.

11 The tree grew large and strong, and its top touched the sky; it was visible to the ends of the earth.

12 Its leaves were beautiful, its fruit abundant, and on it was food for all. Under it the wild animals found shelter, and the birds lived in their branches; from it every creature was fed.

13 "In the visions I saw while lying in bed, I looked, and there before me was a holy one, a messenger, coming down from heaven.

14 He called in a loud voice: 'Cut down the tree and trim off its branches; strip off its leaves and scatter

its fruit. Let the animals flee from under it and the birds from its branches.

15 But let the stump and its roots, bound with iron and bronze, remain in the ground, in the grass of the field. "'Let him be drenched with the dew of heaven and let him live with the animals among the plants of the earth.

16 Let his mind be changed from that of a man and let him be given the mind of an animal, till seven times pass by for him.

17 "'The decision is announced by messengers, the holy ones declare the verdict, so that the living may know that the Most High is sovereign over all kingdoms on earth and gives them to anyone he wishes and sets over them the lowliest of people.'

18 "This is the dream that I, King Nebuchadnezzar, had. Now, Belteshazzar, tell me what it means, for none of the wise men in my kingdom can interpret it for me. But you can because the spirit of the holy gods is in you."

Daniel Interprets the Dream

19 Then Daniel (also called Belteshazzar) was perplexed for a time, and his thoughts terrified him. So, the king said, "Belteshazzar, do not let the dream or its meaning alarm you."

Belteshazzar answered, "My lord, if only the dream applied to your enemies and its meaning to your adversaries!

20 The tree you saw, which grew large and strong, with its top touching the sky, visible to the whole earth,

21 with beautiful leaves and abundant fruit, providing food for all, giving shelter to the wild animals, and having nesting places in its branches for the birds—

22 Your Majesty, you are that tree! You have become great and strong; your greatness has grown until it reaches the sky, and your dominion extends to distant parts of the earth.

23 "Your Majesty saw a holy one, a messenger, coming down from heaven and saying, 'Cut down the tree and destroy it, but leave the stump, bound with iron and bronze, in the grass of the field, while

its roots remain in the ground. Let him be drenched with the dew of heaven; let him live with the wild animals, until seven times pass by for him.'

24 "This is the interpretation, Your Majesty, and this is the decree the Most High has issued against my lord the king:

25 You will be driven away from people and will live with the wild animals; you will eat grass like the ox and be drenched with the dew of heaven. Seven times will pass by for you until you acknowledge that the Highest is sovereign over all kingdoms on earth and gives them to anyone he wishes.

26 The command to leave the stump of the tree with its roots means that your kingdom will be restored to you when you acknowledge that Heaven rules.

27 Therefore, Your Majesty, be pleased to accept my advice: Renounce your sins by doing what is right, and your wickedness by being kind to the oppressed. It may be that then your prosperity will continue."

The Dream Is Fulfilled

28 All this happened to King Nebuchadnezzar.

29 Twelve months later, as the king was walking on the roof of the royal palace of Babylon,

30 he said, "Is not this the great Babylon I have built as the royal residence, by my mighty power and for the glory of my majesty?"

31 Even as the words were on his lips, a voice came from heaven, "This is what is decreed for you, King Nebuchadnezzar: Your royal authority has been taken from you.

32 You will be driven away from people and will live with the wild animals; you will eat grass like the ox. Seven times will pass by for you until you acknowledge that the Most High is sovereign over all kingdoms on earth and gives them to anyone he wishes."

33 Immediately what had been said about Nebuchadnezzar was fulfilled. He was driven away from people and ate grass like the ox. His body was drenched with the dew of heaven until his hair grew like the feathers of an eagle and his nails like the claws of a bird.

34 At the end of that time, I, Nebuchadnezzar, raised my eyes toward heaven, and my sanity was restored. Then I praised the Most High; I honored and glorified him who lives forever. His dominion is an eternal dominion; his kingdom endures from generation to generation.

35 All the peoples of the earth are regarded as nothing. He does as he pleases with the powers of heaven and the peoples of the earth. No one can hold back his hand or say to him: "What have you done?"

36 At the same time that my sanity was restored, my honor and splendor were returned to me for the glory of my kingdom. My advisers and nobles sought me out, and I was restored to my throne and became even greater than before.

37 Now I, Nebuchadnezzar, praise and exalt and glorify the King of heaven, because everything he does is right and all his ways are just. And those who walk with pride can be humble.

Chapter 3: They Are Listening

In Daniel 4 Nebuchadnezzar is giving an account of his deviation of the Truth, and how he redirected himself and reclaimed his life. Please do not disregard the prophetic, the sage nor wise advice of those who God has place in your life. Prophet Daniel told him what to do.

Therefore, Nebuchadnezzar could have avoided the judgment of God. I am providing this narrative to show you what it looks like during many stages of our life when we do not employ repentance.

Below are some symbolic scenarios that we can extract from Nebuchadnezzar experiences:

➢ To the one who has not yet had the dream (warning) remain alert that you do not deceive yourself with a puffed-up ego.

➢ To the one who had the dream and received the interpretation, Remain alert, heed the corrective action and the instructions.

➢ To the one that is at the 11th month, and have not repented, I encourage you to do so. Look around. No matter if you have much or little, it should be important to you to

keep it. Give thanks to God for what you have.

➢ To the one who has reached the 12th month and sentence has been executed, there is still hope. It is possible that you do not have to do the full term of seven years, if you repent.

Nebuchadnezzar repented and acknowledged God as sovereign. In Daniel 4:36-37 it states, "At the same time that my sanity was restored, my honor and splendor were returned to me for the glory of my kingdom. My advisers and nobles sought me out, and I was restored to my throne and became even greater than before. Now I, Nebuchadnezzar, praise and exalt and glorify the King of heaven, because everything he does is right, and all his ways are just. And those who walk with pride can be humble."

God knows our every step and every word we speak. He alone is sovereign. Immediately when Nebuchadnezzar repented, the flicker of life was restored. His sanity, honor, splendor, and the glory of his throne was restored. Nebuchadnezzar's life was greater than before.

> ➤ To the one who completed the Judgment, God loves you and will restore you at the appointed time. He will empowered you to live a successful life.

Life and death are in the Power of our tongue. Therefore, we must speak wisely. The adversary's job is to make us forget who we really are. Fight the good fight of faith and remember to stay alert.

Nebuchadnezzar reclaimed his life by humbling his mind, and God restored him greater than before. We cannot get stuck in who we think we are. We must remain thankful and connected to the Life-Giving Source God himself, the Almighty Himself, the Creator Himself. Look within and let go and let God. We must speak within ourselves and strength our minds/soul to reclaim and redirect our steps. If we are already going in the right direction, stay alert, and stay humble.

Chapter 4: Look Around – You Will See What You Created

In conclusion, let's look at some of the charges that were brought against King Nebuchadnezzar from heaven. Daniel Chapter 3 will help us understand why the charges were brought against Nebuchadnezzar. I want to say as it was then, so it is today. He who has ears let him hear.

Daniel 3:1-6 says, "King Nebuchadnezzar made an image of gold, sixty cubits high and six cubits wide, and set it up on the plain of Dura in the province of Babylon. [2] He then summoned the satraps, prefects, governors, advisers, treasurers, judges, magistrates and all the other provincial officials to come to the dedication of the image he had set up. [3] So the satraps, prefects, governors, advisers, treasurers, judges, magistrates and all the other provincial officials assembled for the dedication of the image that King Nebuchadnezzar had set up, and they stood before it.

[4] Then the herald loudly proclaimed, "Nations and peoples of every language, this is what you are commanded to do: [5] As soon as you hear the sound of the horn, flute, zither, lyre, harp, pipe and all kinds of music, you must fall down and worship the image of gold that King Nebuchadnezzar has set up.

⁶"Whoever does not fall, and worship will immediately be thrown into a blazing furnace."

Below are stages that led up to King Nebuchadnezzar's fall let us stay alert and fear no man, people, place, or thing:

Stage One:

It is usually when the Ego is in the way to cause one to Ignore or is unaware of their Words, Deeds, and Actions.

➢ He made a large IMAGE of gold (God).
➢ He summoned the Leaders to the dedication of the IMAGE of gold.
➢ He uses the art and tools of Music to signal the People.
➢ He demanded the people to worship the Image as it was God.
➢ He threatened the people if they did not worship, they would burn.
➢ He declared himself as God.

Stage Two:

When a warning comes in a form of people, place, or thing we have to pay attention.

The Prophet Daniel interprets the Dream.

Daniel 4:20-26 says, "The tree you saw, which grew large and strong, with its top touching the sky, visible to the whole earth, [21] with beautiful leaves and abundant fruit, providing food for all, giving shelter to the wild animals, and having nesting places in its branches for the birds— [22] Your Majesty, you are that tree! You have become great and strong; your greatness has grown until it reaches the sky, and your dominion extends to distant parts of the earth. [23] "Your Majesty saw a holy one, a messenger, coming down from heaven and saying, 'Cut down the tree and destroy it, but leave the stump, bound with iron and bronze, in the grass of the field, while its roots remain in the ground. Let him be drenched with the dew of heaven; let him live with the wild animals, until seven times pass by for him.' [24] "This is the interpretation, Your Majesty, and this is the decree the Most High has issued against my lord the king". [25] You will be driven away from people and will live with the wild animals; you will eat grass like the ox and be drenched with the dew of heaven. Seven times will pass by for you until you acknowledge that the Highest is sovereign over all kingdoms on earth and gives them to anyone he wishes. [26] The

command to leave the stump of the tree with its roots means that your kingdom will be restored to you when you acknowledge that Heaven rules."

Stage Three:

The Warning came before the destruction, we do not have to suffer mentally, emotionally, or physically.

Daniel 4:27 says, "Therefore, Your Majesty, be pleased to accept my advice: Renounce your sins by doing what is right, and your wickedness by being kind to the oppressed. It may be that then your prosperity will continue."

As you look around and take inventory of your conditions and circumstances, know that this requires stillness and inner strength which we have inherited. We are all in various stages in life. The words we speak give life to our destiny. So, let's be careful of the words we speak.

Stage Four:

When one repents, the reward of repentance is received from the Lord.

Nebuchadnezzar looked around and acknowledged the Sovereignty of God in truth. His repentance moved heaven, and he was restored:

- ➢ His Sanity was restored.

- ➢ His Honor was returned to him.

- ➢ His Splendor was returned to him.

- ➢ He was restored to his throne and became even greater than he was before.

Through all of Nebuchadnezzar experiences he got to the point where he repented and was restored. In turn, he praised and glorified the King of Heaven.

As we reflect, we do not want to forget that everything has ears and everything has a womb. Heaven hears us and we are birthing what we say. So, as we repent and God brings us through, we should not forget to acknowledge and glorify Him as God.

I declare the end from the beginning and ancient times from what is still to come, I say my purpose will stand and all my good pleasure I will accomplish.

Acknowledgement

I would like to thank Dr. Sheldon L Gathers for these impactful words below from his Chancellor.

At all times you must look up!

Excellence is never an accident,

it is always of high intention,

intelligent action,

skillful execution,

and a vision to see obstacles...

as opportunities.

About the Author

Annette **W**ilson is from Chicago, IL, and brings an impressive career spanning over 25 years in Information Technology to her diverse background. Beyond her professional accomplishments, Annette is a devoted Christian teacher of the Word of God and a loving mother to two beautiful adult daughters.

For more than a decade, Annette has dedicated her early mornings to hosting a prayer line, where she nurtures spiritual growth and fosters a strong sense of community. Additionally, she shines as the dynamic host of "Annette's Space," a virtual book club that features insightful interviews with authors and writers, offering readers a captivating journey into the world of literature.

Annette is excited about becoming a first-time author and invite you to come along this journey with her.